Mapping Interdisciplinary Studies

JULIE THOMPSON KLEIN

Published by the
Association of American Colleges and Universities
1818 R Street NW
Washington, DC 20009
www.aacu-edu.org

copyright ©1999

ISBN 0-911696-74-1

Contents

the Academy in Transition

Jerry G. Gaff
SERIES EDITOR

About this series

Convinced that American higher education is in the midst of significant academic changes, AAC&U is launching a new series of occasional papers under the rubric of The Academy in Transition. We recognize that confusion can result from competing calls for change: different voices are demanding new approaches, conflicting agendas are advocated, and the future of higher education is uncertain. The purposes of this series are to analyze changes taking place in key areas of higher education and to provide road maps about the directions and destinations of the changing academy.

The first in this series is *Contemporary Understandings of Liberal Education* by Carol Geary Schneider and Robert Shoenberg. Besides this overview on interdisciplinary education, other papers in preparation include analyses of general education, diversity and learning, education for global understanding, and the intersections of educational quality and cost. As the topics imply, we are convinced that the new academy will interpret traditional concepts of liberal education in contemporary contexts, prize general education more highly, recognize the interrelatedness of disciplines, value the contribution of diversity to quality in education, and incorporate global perspectives as a means for learning, while becoming more cost effective. Collectively, these papers point to a different, more purposeful, robust, and efficient academy that is in the process of being created.

AAC&U encourages faculty members, academic leaders, and all those who care about the future of our colleges and universities to use these papers as a point of departure for their own analyses of the directions of educational change. We hope these essays will encourage academics to think broadly and creatively about the educational communities we inherit, and, by our contributions, the educational communities we want to create.

Acknowledgments

This contribution to The Academy in Transition series is the culmination of a year spent as an AACU Senior Fellow, from 1997-98. The fellowship provided unparalleled access to leading thinkers on the issues that are shaping higher education today. It was also a delightful way of becoming a temporary member of the AAC&U family in Washington, D.C., where everyone extended a warm welcome.

I am grateful to Joe Johnston, Vice President of Educational and Global Initiatives, for suggesting the invitation, and to former AAC&U president Paula P. Brownlee, for making it possible. Both Joe and Jane Spalding, Director of Programs, Office of Education and Global Initiatives, also helped me think about the connections between interdisciplinary studies and international education. The current president, Carol Geary Schneider, continues to provide powerful national support for interdisciplinarity and, along with Debra Humphreys, Director of Programs, Education and Diversity Initiatives helped me think about the connections between interdisciplinarity and diversity.

Iris Jacobs provided support for an AAC&U Network for Academic Renewal meeting on Interdisciplinary Studies in Chicago, including distribution of a preliminary version of this discussion paper. As always, Bridget Puzon, the Academic Editor of *Liberal Education*, also gave valuable editorial advice.

Most of all, I thank Jerry Gaff. With characteristic grace and conviction, Jerry pushed me to to bridge theory and practice in order to serve the needs of the countless faculty and administrators across the country who have made interdisciplinarity the important topic that it is. Jerry's personal and professional friendship is the greatest of treasures reaped from a challenging and invigorating year.

Mapping Interdisciplinary Studies

Metaphors are signs of how we think about the academy. Over the course of the twentieth century, an important set of shifts has occurred in our images of knowledge and education. The metaphor of knowledge as a *foundation* or a *linear structure* has been replaced by images of a *network*, a *web*, and a *dynamic system*. Comparably, the metaphor of unity, with its accompanying values of universality and certainty, has been replaced by metaphors for plurality and relationality in a complex world. Images of the curriculum, in turn, reflect a new emphasis on *integrating, connecting, linking,* and *clustering.* Taken together, these changes signal a major trend. The "Academy in Transition" is an academy that is becoming more interdisciplinary.

Interdisciplinarity became prominent for more than one reason and addresses more than one kind of problem. Disagreements about interdisciplinarity, as a result, often center on differing beliefs about its meaning and purpose. New research and teaching interests have produced a variety of new fields, from molecular biology and material science to cognitive science and policy studies. Moreover, the need for integrative problem solving and teamwork has been a key motivation in the professions, in industry, and in government. These forms of "instrumental interdisciplinarity" differ from efforts to cultivate integrative capacity in general education. They also differ from efforts to restructure knowledge in fields that practice a form of "critical interdisciplinarity," such as women's studies and cultural studies.

Across the country, faculty, administrators, and curriculum committees are keenly aware of a new momentum. Yet, they lack a common understanding of what is happening, and they are even less certain about how to respond. This discussion paper aims to help in two ways. Part I provides an overview of current trends with emphasis on three areas—disciplinary change, interdisciplinary fields, and general education. It answers the question of why interdisciplinarity is taking hold in the academy today. Part II presents talking points for dialogue on key topics of integrating curriculum, integrative process and pedagogies, assessment, faculty development, institutional change, and support strategies. It answers the equally pressing question of how local campuses can respond.

> ... the "Academy in Transition" is an academy that is becoming more interdisciplinary.

Part 1: Mapping

Two books document the current variety of interdisciplinary studies: *Interdisciplinary Undergraduate Programs: A Directory* (Edwards 1996) and *Interdisciplinary Courses and Team Teaching* (Davis 1995). The defining categories of the books are quite similar, and Edwards' data are particularly revealing. In introducing the first directory in 1986, William Newell argued that interdisciplinary education was moving from the "radical fringe to the liberal mainstream." Since then, significant growth has occurred in areas where interdisciplinary study was already strong, especially in women's studies and in general education. Honors programs also remain a prominent site for interdisciplinarity, whether forged in the tradition of liberal education or, like the Honors Program in Mathematical Methods in Social Sciences at Northwestern University, serving specialized purposes.

Despite downsizing and retrenchment, many programs, Edwards found, originated or have been substantially revised since 1986. His most significant finding is the diversi-

"It is clear that interdisciplinary studies are not only alive and well, but are also growing and evolving in new and exciting directions."

— Alan Edwards, Jr.

EDWARDS DIRECTORY OF PROGRAMS	DAVIS SURVEY OF COURSES
• interdisciplinary institutions, cluster colleges	• general education
• majors programs, courses, study groups	• professional and technical programs
• general education, liberal arts/liberal studies	• integrative studies programs
• honors, adult education	• women's/gender studies
• humanities, social sciences, natural science	• multicultural and ethnic studies
• applied science/technology	• international studies
• peace/justice studies	• capstone and integrative courses
• religious/religion studies	• electives
• urban studies	
• film/media studies	
• human development/gerontology	
• science, technology, and society	
• environmental studies, neuroscience	
• American studies, ethnic/cultural/area studies	
• international studies, world/global studies	
• women's/gender studies	
• educational studies/teacher preparation	

fication of the concept. Interdisciplinary fields have developed or expanded dramatically in areas as varied as cognitive science, neuroscience, leadership studies, bioengineering, cultural studies, politics and economics, and philosophy, and teacher education for integrated middle schools. At the same time, informal activities such as faculty study groups have increased as faculty try to keep up with new developments in research. "Interdisciplinary studies," Edwards concluded, "are not only alive and well, but are also growing and evolving in new and exciting directions" (vii, xi-xii).

An even fuller picture emerges from mapping the finer detail of three major areas: disciplines, interdisciplinary fields, and general education.

1. DISCIPLINES

A few decades ago, focusing on disciplines as the first consideration would have seemed contradictory. As fields of inquiry into a particular aspect of the world, disciplines specify the objects studied, the methods and concepts used, the theories accepted, and the assumptions made about what is valid (Messer-Davidow, Shumway, and Sylvan 1993, vii). The long-term trend in the history of undergraduate curriculum has been the growth of specialization and proliferation of programs and courses. At present, though, there is an "historical reversal of this trend" (Gaff and Ratcliff 1997, xiv). Increased crossing of disciplinary boundaries is shifting the defining metaphors of disciplinary practice. In recent disciplinary histories, descriptions of current practices, and reports of professional organizations, traditional images of *depth* and *compartmentalization* are being replaced by images of *boundary crossing* and *cross-fertilization*.

Boundary crossing and cross-fertilization occur for many reasons, though the daily borrowing of tools, methods, concepts, and theories from other disciplines is a major factor. Borrowing skews the picture of knowledge depicted in conventional maps of the academy. Textuality, narrative, and interpretation, for instance, were once thought to *belong* within the *domain* of literary studies. Now they appear across humanities and social sciences, in science studies, and in the professions of law and psychiatry. Likewise, research on the body and on disease occurs in disciplines as varied as art history, gerontology, and biomedicine. The concepts of information and communication are also prominent in media studies, in social psychology, and in engineering.

Clifford Geertz (1980) suggested a metaphor that explains this phenomenon—*migration*. The movement of methods and analytical approaches across disciplinary boundaries has become an important feature of knowledge production today. The intellectual scene is replete with examples—in studies of family systems, children, gender, culture, language, the body, the mind, and the evolution of the earth. As a result, the majority of fields today have what Schneider calls a certain "multidisciplinary" thrust, whether deemed "disciplinary" or "interdisciplinary" (1997, 238).

Giles Gunn's description of literary studies is rich in metaphors of interdisciplinarity. "The threading of disciplinary principles," he found, "is frequently doubled, tripled, and quadrupled, in ways that are not only mixed, but, from a conventional disciplinary perspective, somewhat off center." They are characterized by *overlapping, underlayering, interlacing, crosshatching affiliations, coalitions,* and *alliances.* "The inevitable result of much interdisciplinary study, if not its ostensible purpose, is to dispute and disorder conventional understandings of the relations between such things as origin and terminus, center and periphery, focus and margin, inside and outside" (1992, 249).

The gap between the *cutting edge* or *frontier* of research and the curriculum is well known. Jerry Gaff, however, likens scholarship to the *molten mass of radioactive material* that forms the core of the earth. Periodically it erupts in a *volcano* or shifts *tectonic plates* (1997, 701). As a result of both slow change and dramatic developments, the major is changing.

The first national report on the major emanated from a three-year study by twelve learned societies, sponsored by AAC&U (1990-92). Some disciplines have been more responsive than others. Literary studies and political science, for example, have been more receptive to interdisciplinary change than philosophy and economics, although all disciplines are grappling with the *knowledge explosion* and *fragmentation* of the curriculum. The twelve learned societies were unanimous in calling for greater coherence in the major as well as connection making with other disciplines and the world beyond the academy.

As links with other disciplines and interdisciplinary fields become more visible, project organizers suggest, the metaphor of a major shifts from a *silo* to a *matrix* of connections and relations. Connection making ranges from adding new courses and concentrations to completely restructuring a major. Senior capstone courses have been a particularly effective means of achieving a greater sense of coherence and relationality both in the major and in general education. Recent state-of-the-art accounts of disciplines in the *Handbook of the Undergraduate Curriculum* (1997) yield added evidence of change.

Humanities. In surveying changes in humanities disciplines between 1985 and 1995, Lyn Maxwell White found that course design, content, and approaches have become more collaborative across departments, and traditional viewpoints are being merged with new scholarship and diverse perspectives. Content has broadened to include more comparative

"...the inevitable result of much interdisciplinary study, if not its ostensible purpose, is to dispute and disorder conventional understandings of the relations between such things as origin and terminus, center and periphery, focus and margin, inside and outside."
— Giles Gunn

study, informed by new scholarship on the complex dynamics of culture. Poststructuralist theories of language and meaning, coupled with new understandings of the nature of texts and reading, have changed classroom approaches to traditional and new texts and subjects. Similarly, model humanities programs in the Edwards directory span a range of interests, from traditional studies of Western culture and historical periods to new approaches to religious studies, women's and gender studies, and applied ethics.

As curricula become increasingly connected and integrated, boundary lines become harder to draw; for example, scholarship in English is incorporating approaches from history, philosophy, and anthropology. Meanwhile, scholars in historical studies are borrowing quantitative methods from sociology and using narrative and interpretive strategies developed in literary studies. Humanistic and scientific methods are also being used to examine subject matter in interdisciplinary core curricula and in fields such as environmental studies. For example, Southwest Texas State University, an interdisciplinary and intercultural regional studies curriculum focuses on the relationship of the region's geography and physical ecology to its history and the interaction of Anglo, Chicano, and Native American cultures. The program is a two-semester upper division minor that includes a laboratory.

Social Sciences. In the social sciences, Hendershott and Wright found a variety of interrelations with humanities, sciences, and general education. New alliances are being forged in interdisciplinary courses at the same time that increased interdisciplinarity in some disciplines, such as psychology and sociology, has resulted in hybrid fields. Some of the most creative innovations couple one or more social sciences with natural and health sciences, humanities, education, and professions. These new disciplinary partnerships focus on complex social problems such as crime, juvenile violence, infant mortality, AIDS, ethnic tensions, and pollution.

Boundary crossing is often accompanied by disputes over academic *turf.* The location of ethnic studies and gender studies majors in English or literary studies departments, for instance, has rekindled debate on the "proper" domains of social science and of humanities. AAC&U's project on "Engaging Cultural Legacies" transcended traditional humanities-based conceptions of culture to include social sciences and resulted in new courses and dialogue among faculty from different disciplines.

Natural Sciences. In the natural sciences, Wubbels and Girgus also found a variety of developments. In addition to focusing courses on complex problems and topics and exploring the relationship of science and society, faculty are designing curricula that reflect the blurring of boundaries in contemporary research. The University of

Pennsylvania devised a new introductory course that integrates mathematics, physics, and chemistry, while Rensselaer Polytechnic Institute conceived a joint biochemistry and biophysics program that integrates physics, chemistry, and biology courses. New interdisciplinary fields and technologies are also being incorporated. The University of Wisconsin developed a course in general chemistry based on the context of physical materials, while "Stanford University developed project-based laboratories for general chemistry curriculum using lasers" (*Handbook*, 294).

A new major at Western Michigan University offers an extended illustration. Like faculty in other disciplines, members of the department of biological sciences were responding to changes in research and educational reforms. They redesigned the major into a new program that emphasizes more integrative courses highlighted by asterisks in the table below. At the introductory level, students focus on conceptual mapping of complex environmental problems, with emphasis on stimulating inquiry and developing vocabulary. At the middle level, courses focus on information and conceptual frameworks that concern both the natural world and the world of human institutions. At the senior level, all majors have a capstone experience. In addition to reformulating the biology major, Western Michigan developed an environmental studies program that likewise includes a capstone experience (AAC&U 1994, *Changing the Major*, 18-19).

Hybrids. The creation of hybrid interdisciplinary specializations also marks another shift in boundaries, toward more problem-centered and competence-based structures.

BIOLOGY MAJOR
Western Michigan University

Level	Previous Major	Reformed Major
Introductory	Animal Biology	Molecular/Cellular*
	Plant Biology	Evolutionary/Organismal*
	Cell Biology	Genetics*
Intermediate	Genetics	Microbiology or Botany
	Physiology	Physiology (Plant or Human)
	Ecology	Ecology
Advanced	3 courses from unrestricted list	2 courses from cluster groups
Capstone	None	Capstone Experience
Total Hours	36	34

This development, James Farmer speculates, may signal a gradual but profound shift in the organizational paradigm of higher education, away from the primary context of disciplines to knowledge restructured by application. Chemistry, he forecasts, will be applied increasingly to subsets of medicine or engineering. A student will study biology and chemistry as they apply to health care or chemical engineering, not biology and chemistry per se. Already, one university curriculum in blood-bank technology is combining courses in chemistry, biology, health sciences, and business. The needs and priorities of blood banks are the primary focus, not the disciplines per se. At one technology institute, the packaging design curriculum includes art, photography, printing, business, and design in courses geared toward the study of design and production of packaging for consumer products (*Handbook*, 477, 490). At another university, the physics department developed a new audio technology program to train students in the technology of sound and electronic recording for careers in mass media and in the entertainment industry.

Indicative of overlapping interests in an academy marked by plurality and complexity, many changes in the disciplines are linked with the second major area of activity, interdisciplinary fields.

2. INTERDISCIPLINARY FIELDS

Interdisciplinary fields, Douglas Bennett suggests, comprise one of six major frontiers of innovation (1997). Their emergence is not a new phenomenon. In the 1940s, American studies and area studies emerged. In the 1960s and 1970s, women's studies, environmental studies, and urban studies entered the academy. In the closing decade of the century, interdisciplinary fields are greater in number and visibility: Since 1945, many new fields have been hybrid in nature, and, in the closing decade of the century, interdisciplinary fields are greater in number and visibility. By 1987, there were 8,530 definable knowledge fields (Crane and Small 1992, 197). The metaphor of a *knowledge explosion* signifies a major reason.

In large and even mid-sized institutions, it is not unusual to find a number of fields, including the following typical examples:

- women's, African-American, and ethnic studies
- local, regional, and American cultural studies
- area and international studies
- urban, legal, labor, and peace and conflict studies
- medieval, renaissance, and Victorian studies and comparative literature
- gerontology, criminology, and policy studies

- information science, cognitive science, communication and media studies
- materials science and molecular biology

All interdisciplinary fields are not the same. American studies and social psychology, for example, have had different trajectories from molecular biology and policy studies. A field of study has a different character from campus to campus. Its broad intellectual development is a major factor in its legitimation. Yet, the political economy and institutional culture of a campus is often a greater factor in its local identity and influence. On one campus a field may enjoy all the perks, on another it may struggle for survival. On one campus, faculty may have the freedom to pursue interdisciplinary interests, on another they may find their work devalued in the reward system.

Program structures likewise vary across a range of size and formality:
- augmented specializations within existing departments
- coordinated multidisciplinary studies, linking courses in traditional departments
- interdisciplinary programs with introductory and capstone seminars and theses
- concentrations within larger interdisciplinary programs
- freestanding departments, centers, or schools.

All interdisciplinary fields are enclaves for new research and curricular innovations. "Multidisciplinary identity fields," however, work toward a different end than fields focused on economic and technological problems. Identity fields represent, Bennett (1997, 144) suggests, a "sacred edge" in the reopened battle over inclusion and exclusion. One of their shared goals is to *reconfigure* the social and cognitive space of the academy into a new *community of pluralities* that is both intercultural and interdisciplinary (Humphreys 1997, xi, 31-32, 40). Newly emerging fields have been vital to the project of interrupting and revivifying older ones. They also signal the growth of a "new academy" around the edges and, increasingly, within the departments of the "old academy."

AAC&U's American Commitments National Panel defined the new academy as a composite of new ways of thinking and forms of scholarship, reconfigurations of disciplines, new modes of teaching and assessment, and a relational pluralism. As new fields and pedagogies intersect with disciplinary and general education, the "liberal arts of translation" across the curriculum are being enacted. The relational learning fostered by these arts gives students the abilities, commitments, and knowledge they need to move among subjects and fields, individuals, communities, cultures, and nations. Students gain an understanding of how differences in a complex world are mediated through relations, mutual transactions, and dialogical connections (Minnich 1995).

Relational pluralism is further evident in the spatial dynamics of interdisciplinary fields. One of the major effects of interdisciplinary fields—cross-fertilization of the curriculum—occurs because they assume multiple forms and appear at multiple sites.

Diversity, for instance, tends to appear in three curricular options:

- specialized courses from new interdisciplinary fields (international, regional, American ethnic, Third World, and women's studies)
- theory, content, and pedagogy from ethnic, women's and area studies incorporated into courses fulfilling general education requirements
- new interdisciplinary courses in the upper division focusing on the multiplicity of cultural experiences, through either a menu of courses under a single rubric with common elements or one course with multiple sections (Olguin & Schmitz 1997, 449)

International interests, likewise, appear across the curriculum:

- The intersection of some fields—international studies, area studies, peace or world order studies—are explicitly devoted to examining international or global questions.
- Certain disciplines—geography and anthropology—are intrinsically international in concern.
- Still other disciplines—archaeology, botany, geology, linguistics, zoology, entomology, and comparative specialties in social sciences and humanities—extend their knowledge bases in direct proportion to access to new sites and materials (Johnston and Spalding 1997, 423; Groennings 1990)

These examples underscore another defining characteristic of the academy in transition. It is a both/and world, not an either/or world. The *revolution* embodied in women's studies, for example, has occurred outside, across, and within the disciplines. New insights, knowledge, and experience challenged the existing knowledge base, *breaking down barriers* between disciplines and encouraging exploration of *unifying* themes, concepts, and forces. Feminist scholarship, Catharine Stimpson explains, is less a single map than a "portfolio of maps." The effects are likewise plural. In establishing the unreliability of other knowledge maps, scholars, teachers, and students have *charted* new knowledge territory and heightened reflection on all *mapmaking* (1992, 251). Research and curriculum have been *restructured* around topics such as the history of women, the philosophy of gender, knowledge construction, the economic realities of women, and the biologies of sexuality. The field also provides a ground for liberating dialogue intended to impart new social and personal relevance (García and Ratcliff, 119-20; Musil, 206).

Reflecting the complexity of today's academy, a single reform may be a multitiered response to disciplinary change, a pertinent interdisciplinary field, and a local mission. In transforming the English Department into a School of Literature, Communication, and Culture (LCC), Georgia Institute of Technology developed a new bachelor's degree in Science, Technology, and Culture (STAC), plus a new minor on Women, Science, and Technology. Designed for students in a technology-oriented institution, the new major addresses needs they will face in their careers. It also incorporates one of the most important developments in the field of science, technology, and society studies—the confluence of communication, science, technology, and culture. The popular image of interdisciplinary programs, Department Co-Chair Alan Rauch (1997) emphasizes, often fails to encompass the sophisticated dissolution of disciplinary boundaries embodied in this kind of curricular reform. In addition, it moves beyond a simple dichotomy of instrumental versus critical interdisciplinarity to create an integration of problem solving and critical perspectives.

Many other fields, including computer science and ecology, crossed disciplinary boundaries to test knowledge bases and modes of inquiry (Ratcliff, 144). Fields as varied as policy analysis, women's studies, and environmental studies both model and require a convergence of problem-centered, multidisciplinary, and integrative approaches to learning (Schneider and Shoenberg 1997, 15). They also respond to student needs. The Neuroscience Program at Trinity College (CT) was established in 1990 in recognition of needs perceived from previous student-designed interdisciplinary majors in the field. "Far ahead of faculty with their innovative views," Ann Ferren reminds us, "many students do not hold sacred the disciplinary boundaries and want to combine fields such as design, communication, computer science or business, languages, and area studies" (1997, 545).

**DEPARTMENT OF NEUROSCIENCE
BROWN UNIVERSITY**

- **8 background courses in math, physics, biomed, chemistry or biochemistry, and computer science**
- **3 neuroscience introductory courses**
- **2 neuroscience laboratory courses**
- **4 additional courses chosen in a topical emphasis, such as cellular and molecular neuroscience, systems neuroscience, behavioral neuroscience, or computational neuroscience**

The department of neuroscience at Brown University illustrates a new relationality of disciplines and interdisciplinary interests. The department offers a seventeen-course concentration in areas of knowledge important to understanding brain function. Founded in 1977, the department brings together neurobiology (anatomy, physiology, biochemistry, molecular biology, and genetics), with psychology and cognitive science, and with mathematical and physical principles involved in modeling neural systems. The concentration allows students flexibility to develop their final two years along lines of individual preference. To receive a degree with honors, students must also complete independent research.

Although motivations differ, all interdisciplinary fields raise the same question: Where do they fit? The metaphor of *fit*, Lynton Caldwell observed, prejudges the epistemological problem at stake in the emergence of fields such as environmental studies. Many new fields arose because of a perceived *misfit* among need, experience, information, and the structuring of knowledge and curriculum embodied *in disciplinary organization*. The implications are profound. If the structure of the academy must be changed to accommodate the new field, perhaps the structure itself is part of the problem. Interdisciplinary studies, Caldwell asserts, are not mere additions to the curriculum. They represent "a latent and fundamental restructuring of knowledge and formal education" (1983, 247-49).

Restructuring is no less apparent in the third major area and one of the greatest growth sectors of interdisciplinary studies, general education.

3. GENERAL EDUCATION

In a discussion paper in this series, *General Education: The Changing Agenda*, Jerry Gaff (1999) identifies integration of knowledge as a major trend today. Integration overlaps with other trends, underscoring the growing importance of relational learning. The most prominent interdisciplinary practices in general education today are designing integrated alternatives to traditional distribution models, insuring breadth of knowledge, clustering and linking courses, building learning communities, and incorporating diver-sity, new interdisciplinary knowledges, and new pedagogics.

General education is often viewed as a route to solving more than one problem. Organizational sociologists call this tendency the "garbage can phenomenon." An assortment of problems is thrown into one vessel. If they can't be carted away, the hope is their mixture will suggest a next step (Civian, et al., 652). Creating an integrative curriculum requires more than just *tinkering*. Instead of simply *adding* or *jettisoning* courses, integrative learning calls for *revisioning* and *restructuring*.

Rather than clinging to the impossible model of coverage, reforms foster greater *coherence* and *connection*. In a world where "Nobody can do everything anymore," as one faculty member said, integration is more important than ever.

Cluster and *community* are prominent metaphors of interdisciplinary reform. Grouping separate disciplinary courses and linking them with a discussion session or a seminar shifts the logic of curriculum from a *distribution* model that sends students across the campus map in search of dispersed general education credits, to the logic of *integration*. University Studies at Portland State University incorporates several features of current reforms.

First, a large distribution of fifty-four credits selected from different departments has been replaced with a more streamlined and integrative approach, anchored by theme-based, team-organized integrative seminars. These seminars cultivate the capacity to examine new areas of learning holistically, critically, and reflectively. Second, the choice of two diversity courses from a list has been replaced with the option of courses selected from either interdisciplinary programs or course clusters that provide multiple pathways through the curriculum.

The most prominent interdisciplinary practices in general education today are:

- **designing alternatives to distribution models**
- **insuring breadth of knowledge**
- **clustering and linking courses**
- **building learning communities**
- **incorporating diversity**
- **incorporating new interdisciplinary fields**
- **incorporating new pedagogies**

Third, instead of three designated courses (two in English composition and one in health education), students in the junior or senior year continue to select an interdisciplinary program or a general education cluster. Fourth, the program culminates in a Senior Capstone Experience that features community-based projects. Working in teams, students cultivate problem-solving and collaborative skills. Fifth, academic skills are integrated within course content, and diversity and multicultural themes are included across the curriculum (Reardon and Ramaley 1997, 525-31).

Over the past two decades, learning communities have become increasingly popular means of fostering *connection* and *collaboration*. By definition, though, learning communities rearrange curricular time and space around common themes. Not all formats are interdisciplinary. Courses are *clustered* in pairs or threes, in programs of coordinated studies, and in rarer cases, such as Evergreen State College, the *raison d'etre* of an entire institution (Matthews, et al. 1997, 457-58). A glance across the map illustrates the variety of settings:

- The oldest model, the Federated Learning Communities at SUNY-Stony Brook, clusters existing courses around themes such as World Hunger and Social and Ethical Issues in the Life Sciences. The addition of a new faculty member, a "master learner," assures comparative reflection across courses.

- All first-year students in Lee Honors College at Western Michigan University

GENERAL EDUCATION PROGRAM

Portland State University

PREVIOUS REQUIREMENTS	NEW REQUIREMENTS
BASIC (54 cr.): 18 credits from each of 3 disciplines in 2 departments per area; 18 must be upper division	FRESHMAN INQUIRY: Three 5-credit courses (15 cr.)
DIVERSITY COURSEWORK 2 courses from an approved list from 2 departments (6 cr., may be included in the 54-cr. above)	SOPHOMORE YEAR (12 cr.) Three 4-credit courses selected from different interdisciplinary programs or general education cluster
WRITING 121 (3 cr.)	JUNIOR or SENIOR YEARS (12 cr.) Complete 1 interdisciplinary program or general education cluster (four 3-credit courses)
WRITING 323 (3 cr.)	
PHE 295 (3 cr.)	SENIOR CAPSTONE (6 credits)
(Minimum: 63 credits)	(Minimum: 45 credits)

take 2- or 3-credit clusters that connect to general education requirements. More than a dozen communities are offered each year. One of them, Peoples of the World, clusters courses in English, anthropology, and geography.

- The Interdisciplinary Learning Communities Project at the State University of New York College at Potsdam offers paired, clustered, and linked courses. Students may self-design interdisciplinary majors. Organized clusters include studies in education, pre-law, and a link with an Adirondacks environmental studies program.

Interdisciplinarity has also gained heightened visibility as a result of addressing the needs of a wider range of students. The traditional assumption about college has been that students live and study together for four years. An increasing percentage of students today, however, are commuters, part-timers, or adult learners who attend class during evenings and in satellite locations. Moreover, half of the students in higher education—in some states even more—are attending community colleges. Creating a sense of community among these students, formerly thought impossible, is not only possible; it is all the more important in such settings.

La Guardia Community College offers early and ongoing clusters in liberal arts. One 11-credit cluster of team-planned courses combines writing with two courses in the social sciences or humanities. Later, a one-credit integrating seminar was added. Students travel as a group to all courses in the cluster. At Lower Columbia College in

Washington, a Learning Communities program provides connections between separate course outcomes in arts and sciences. In addition, an Integrative Studies program features theme-based study, and Linked Studies couples theme-based studies with a writing component.

Diversity is as important a metaphor as *community*. Unities in a plural world are made, not found. James Ratcliff makes a pertinent distinction between consistency and coherence: Consistency implies absence of contradiction; coherence allows for many kinds of connection. Coherence is also an "evolving social construct," not a "linear framework." The difference is apparent in the way an institution deals with multiculturalism. Understood as an added imperative, multiculturalism complicates the curriculum; it is a contradiction. Understood as a task in integration and coherence, it does not mean simply adding to a curriculum or creating a false unity. it requires constructing a logical sequencing (1997).

The relational pluralism of diversity also echoes the nature of interdisciplinary knowledge. Working across disciplines is a form of "intercultural communication," because it requires working with multiple perspectives. This idea is put into practice in the Cultural Encounters program at St. Lawrence University, an alternative means of fulfilling the breadth component of the university's general education requirement.

An influential model, the Cultural Encounters program features a two-course track, with possibilities for study abroad, and a senior capstone seminar. All core components include both western and non-western subject matter, and they are writing intensive. In addition, the program addresses the relatedness of international education to domestic pluralism. Directors of the program, Grant Cornwell and Eve Stoddard, prefer the term interculturalism to "multiculturalism" or "diversity" because it captures the comparative searching and critical dialogue at the heart of the program and the differences that shape all cultural relations (Johnston and Spalding 1997, 432; Cornwell and Stoddard 1994, 1998).

Interdisciplinarity is further legitimated by evidence of positive effects. The learning communities at LaGuardia Community College have yielded tangible proof that retention and degree completion are favorably affected. At Portland State University, which was facing declining retention rates and budgetary shortfalls, retention of first-year students and applications for the first year increased significantly. In a more subtle but no less significant effect, the St. Lawrence program has created an alternative faculty culture on campus, characterized by the same kind of enrichment that faculty on other campuses report resulting from interdisciplinary teaching.

THE CULTURAL ENCOUNTERS PROGRAM

St. Lawrence University

FIRST COURSE

"Level One: Conceiving the World" is a comparative introduction to several cultures focused on topical dimensions of human experience, such as death, work, gender, and healing.

SECOND COURSE

"Level Two: Cultural Encounters" is organized historically, with emphasis on multiplicity and cultural diffusion. It introduces concepts of hegemony, colonialism, appropriation, and resistance and focuses on how cultures change through contact with other cultures.

STUDY ABROAD EXPERIENCE

Prepared for in the Second Course

SENIOR SEMINAR

The seminar examines contemporary global issues such as hunger, AIDS, the environment, and peace. Students reflect critically on how their studies, both abroad and on campus, have enlarged their perspectives and increased their knowledge.

FOREIGN LANGUAGE STUDY

An additional two semesters of a language.

The challenge of responding to interdisciplinary change is even more daunting than mapping it. The following talking points are intended to provide a common vocabulary and framework for discussing, formulating, and implementing change.

Part II: Responding

Informed action requires familiarity with the literature and the best thinking about:

- integrating curriculum
- integrative process
- integrating faculty
- interdisciplinary pedagogies
- assessment
- institutional change
- political strategies

Any curriculum must make sense locally. Yet, to achieve quality, it must also be informed by research and the national conversation. Enlightened change requires familiarity with the literature on interdisciplinarity and the best thinking about seven major topics: integrating curriculum, integrative process, faculty development, interdisciplinary pedagogies, assessment, institutional change, and support strategies.

Klein and Newell (1997) define interdisciplinary studies as a "process of answering a question, solving a problem, or addressing a topic that is too broad or complex to be dealt with adequately by a single discipline or profession." The heart of interdisciplinarity is the *interplay* of perspectives that occurs in balancing depth, breadth, and synthesis. Depth insures the necessary disciplinary, professional, and interdisciplinary knowledge and information for the task at hand. Breadth insures a multidisciplinary variety of perspectives. Synthesis insures integrative process and construction of a holistic perspective that is greater than the simple sum of its parts (393-394, 404-407).

A variety of strategies promote integration (see table below).

The rate and complexity of knowledge growth means that frequent and even continuous curriculum redesign is becoming increasingly necessary (Farmer 1997, 480). This

STRATEGIES FOR INTEGRATING CURRICULUM

- organizing courses around a topic, theme, issue, idea, problem, or question
- designing introductory and senior capstone seminars, theses, and projects
- clustering disciplinary courses around a particular theme or field of interests
- linking disciplinary courses with integrative seminars or discussion groups
- devising courses and units that reflect on the process of integration
- engaging in team teaching
- building learning communities

- using particular integrative approaches, such as systems theory, feminism, and textualism
- giving students models of interdisciplinary knowledge and integrative process
- requiring integrative portfolios
- offering residential living-learning experiences
- fostering interdisciplinary approaches to fieldwork, internships, travel-study, and service learning

development places a higher burden on faculty development. Older models, however, do not suffice. Faculty development today means more than just keeping up with one discipline, though even doing that requires familiarity with interdisciplinary developments. Faculty also need capabilities for teaching in general education as well as working with primary sources, quantitative reasoning, new technologies, and new pedagogies. In addition, they need to cultivate skills for teaching theme- and problem-based courses, core courses, and senior seminars, projects, and theses (Civian et al., 664).

A variety of strategies promote interdisciplinary faculty development (see accompanying table).

One of the most frequent questions faculty ask regards the nature of interdisciplinary pedagogy. While there is no unique pedagogy, innovative approaches that promote dialogue and community, higher-order critical thinking, and problem solving are common; they also tend to be student centered. Many educators consider team teaching to be synonymous with interdisciplinary studies, but there is more team planning than actual team teaching. The appropriate metaphor, James Davis suggests, is *inventing* the curriculum. Although model syllabi and programs are valuable and should be consulted, interdisciplinary study is creative and constructed rather than imitative and formulaic. The active nature of interdisciplinary pedagogy is apparent in the most common approaches (see

STRATEGIES FOR FACULTY DEVELOPMENT

- offering summer and academic-year seminars, workshops, and colloquia
- including interdisciplinary interests in existing faculty development programs and the programming of teaching and learning centers
- using the existing system of seed money to stimulate interdisciplinary curriculum and research development
- channeling indirect costs and overhead from external grants to create new seed grants
- using sabbatical leaves for interdisciplinary research and curriculum development
- traveling to meetings of interdisciplinary organizations and programs at other institutions
- participating in ongoing and special institutes, workshops, and meetings
- hiring consultants and administrators
- holding regular meetings of interdisciplinary course and program faculty
- scheduling retreats and faculty work days
- encouraging informal study groups, teaching circles, and research networks
- engaging in annual and bi-annual course and program review
- building and maintaining course and program portfolios for faculty
- mentoring, peer coaching, visiting each other's courses, and team teaching
- building interdisciplinary resource collections in the library and in program offices

INTERDISCIPLINARY PEDAGOGIES

- plenary lectures coupled with discussion groups or workshops
- team teaching and team planning
- collaborative learning among students and with teachers
- joint research projects and learning communities
- discussion techniques featuring groupwork, freewriting, dyads and triads
- constructivist models of teaching and learning
- inquiry- and discovery-based learning
- experiential and service learning
- game and role playing, case study method
- use of portfolios
- proactive attention to integration and synthesis

accompanying table).

Cornwell and Stoddard (forthcoming) add an important insight. In interdisciplinary teaching, pedagogy becomes more intentional. Interdisciplinary structures become sites of "transformative faculty development," because they are laboratories for innovative pedagogy, new coalitions, and expanded research and teaching interests. Trends in interdisciplinary teaching are also related to a larger shift in thinking about teaching and learning across the academy. This shift is indicated by the move from images of production, prescription, control, performance, mastery, and expertise to images of dialogue, process, inquiry, transformation, interaction, construction, and negotiation.

Emphasis on learning process, in turn, shifts the metaphor of teaching from *telling* to *mentoring* from "sage on the stage" to "guide on the side."

Bill Newell (forthcoming) adds a final observation. Interdisciplinary study is one example of a more fundamental process of "integrative study." Interdisciplinary studies by definition involve more than one discipline, and a variety of approaches cultivates integrative understanding. They include learning communities, collaborative learning, residential communities, experiential learning, and study abroad. The heightened presence of interdisciplinarity in the curriculum is due, in no small part, to the productive intersections of interdisciplinarity and integrative approaches. They cultivate capacities for question posing, decision making, problem solving, and integration and synthesis. They also utilize familiar skills of information gathering and organizing, comparing and contrasting, analyzing and synthesizing. Three additional issues—assessment, institutional change, and support strategies—loom large across interdisciplinary studies of all types.

ASSESSMENT

Until recently, the question of interdisciplinary assessment did not have a clear-cut answer. Lacking clear guidelines, faculty and administrators tried to make do with—or worse, had to conform to—discipline-based measures. The work that is currently being done not only defines unique conditions of interdisciplinary assessment, it overlaps with a wider shift in thinking about assessment across higher education. The traditional view of assessment privileged tests as proof that a student has command of key concepts and skills. New work on assessment is emphasizing performance over recognition and recall. Three broad shifts have occurred: from quantitative to qualitative approaches, from summative to formative evaluation, and from reliance on inputs to emphasis on outcomes (Farmer and Napieralski 1997).

> **DESIRED OUTCOMES IN INTERDISCIPLINARY PROGRAMS**
>
> • **greater tolerance of ambiguity and paradox**
>
> • **sensitivity to ethical dimensions of issues**
>
> • **ability to synthesize or integrate**
>
> • **ability to demythologize experts**
>
> • **humility and sensitivity to bias**
>
> • **enlarged perspectives or horizons**
>
> • **critical thinking and unconventional thinking**
>
> • **empowerment**
>
> • **creativity and original insights**
>
> • **ability to balance subjective and objective thinking**

Interdisciplinary assessment is complicated by the diversity of curricula and the complexity of the task. By definition, more than one discipline is involved. Each carries specific and sometimes conflicting assumptions about assessment. Quality of integration must also be evaluated, and innovative pedagogies often call for new ways of assessing as well. When a task force affiliated with the Association for Integrative Studies examined learning claims and desired outcomes, process emerged as the primary focus, not content.

In the first sustained discussion of the topic, Field, Lee, and Field (1994) emphasized that interdisciplinary programs, by their very nature, are unique. No standard curriculum supplies a universal index. Many faculty, in fact, question whether acquisition of knowledge is a primary goal. Lack of a standard curriculum may well be a major advantage, since it focuses attention on development of intellectual capability, not a fixed body of information. Intellectual maturation and cognitive development become appropriate conceptual frameworks for assessment.

The key to appropriate assessment, Karl Schilling (forthcoming) emphasizes, is "'listening to the sounds of the curriculum." Descriptive assessment provides a fuller picture of what is going on. Standardized tests, or parts of such tests, may be relevant in a particular context. Quality, however, is a multidimensional concept. Quantitative approaches alone cannot get at the intellectual complexity and the discovery-orientation of much of interdisciplinary study. Consequently, an appropriate assessment plan employs multiple methods, including locally designed and qualitative measures. In surveying approaches to assessment in a variety of programs, Field, Lee, and Field (71-75) found comparable tendencies:

• At the School of Interdisciplinary Studies at Miami University (OH), faculty relied initially on nationally normed tests but moved increasingly to qualitative measures, such as portfolio analysis. They also now rely on faculty interviews, pre- and post-testing using ACT COMP, and a nationally normed questionnaire measuring students' self-reports. Information on graduate-school exams and admissions plus a nationally normed alumni assessment instrument provide external data.

- At Evergreen State College, assessment began with existing data on cognitive development of first-year students and on self-evaluations. Pre- and post-testing using the Measure of Intellectual Development instrument measures progress in cognitive development. Retrospective studies of students employ narrative self evaluations.
- Wayne State University's Interdisciplinary Studies Program (ISP) maintains a developmental approach and relies on locally developed instruments. Entry-level holistic and standardized instruments are combined with self assessment of educational goals. These activities begin in an introductory seminar on the nature of interdisciplinary studies. Ongoing assessment activities include portfolios, writing-intensive experiences, and improved data collection

Even though development and maturation are primary foci, content is obviously not irrelevant. To date, few interdisciplinary fields have articulated their views of assessment. Women's studies is an exception. In *Students at the Center,* Caryn McTighe Musil (1992) collected results of a lengthy study conducted by AAC&U and the National Women's Studies Association. Researchers expected that standardized tests would dominate, but they found a variety of assessment methods and a sophisticated conception of assessment. The general emphasis was on improving over proving, student experience over time instead of a single measurement, and multiple methods and sources of information. Because feminist pedagogy is heavily shaped by feminist knowledge and informed by relationships between teachers and students, a variety of quantitative and qualitative approaches is being used. Feminist assessment is also student-centered, participatory, and affected by local context or institutional cultures.

When building an assessment plan, Bill Moore, Coordinator of Student Outcomes

BUILDING AN ASSESSMENT PLAN

- **Articulate goals for assessment early in the process of developing a plan**
- **Compare program goals with goals of the larger institution and pertinent professional groups**
- **Combine multiple methods and perspectives, both quantitative and qualitative**
- **Utilize locally designed qualitative approaches**
- **Utilize standard instruments (or parts) that measure pertinent goals in a contextualized manner**
- **Incorporate feedback loops that lead back to improvements in teaching**
- **Begin with a few potentially useful assessment activities**
- **Engage in ongoing data collection.**

Assessment for the Washington State Board for Community and Technical Colleges, urges all educators to "Think big, but start small." Starting with small empirical approaches is a sounder strategy than constructing an elaborate conceptual approach. An organic approach allows for contextualization and growth. Good assessment, Moore emphasizes, is also grounded in good classroom practice. Hence, it is inseparable from teaching/learning processes.

The most compelling advice—that any plan must be contextualized locally—also applies to the final issues, institutional change and support strategies.

INSTITUTIONAL CHANGE AND SUPPORT STRATEGIES

An old saw comes to mind: Trying to change a curriculum is more difficult than trying to move a cemetery. Curriculum is an inherently fractious arena in which people play out differing intellectual, social, and political agendas. One administrator, emerging from a lengthy effort to create a new general education program, lamented, "This isn't a curriculum. It's a peace treaty." Even at the outset, when hopes run high, a lot is on the line. Another administrator, embarking on a major revision of undergraduate education on campus, admitted, "If we blow this, it'll be another twenty years before we can try again."

Increased interdisciplinarity has heightened the legitimacy of new fields and approaches, but change can still be difficult. Faculty may already feel overburdened, and interdisciplinarity runs counter to traditional ways of thinking, behaving, planning, and budgeting in many institutions (Civian et al., 630, 676; Gaff, 695). Change is further impeded by disputed histories. On one campus, proponents of expanding interdisciplinary programs were opposed by faculty who cited an earlier failure. After searching through the fog of institutional amnesia, they realized the program in question never really existed. They also discovered a huge gulf in impressions. Opponents argued against interdisciplinary change, contending that disciplines were the foundation stones of the university. Proponents argued they were losing potential faculty, especially younger candidates, to universities that offered greater opportunities to do interdisciplinary work in their disciplines and in new fields.

In trying to stimulate change, participants need to recognize that a number of intervening variables are at work (Klein and Newell, 400-401). Each variable should be identified and weighed (see table on page 22).

In addition to considering these variables, participants should also discuss their philosophies of change. Reflecting different beliefs about the nature and purpose of interdisciplinarity, disputes about curricular reform often center on conflicting beliefs about whether change should *modify* or *transform* a campus.

CONCEPTUAL AND ORGANIZATIONAL VARIABLES

- **nature of the institution: size, mission, and financial base**
- **institutional culture: prior experience with curricular reform, patterns of interaction among faculty and administration, nature of the academic community, local knowledge cultures, assumptions about learning styles of students**
- **the nature and level of the desired change: institution-wide, program-wide, or a single course; general education, majors, or concentrations, department or program enhancement, learning communities**
- **requirements of the change: modification of existing structures or creation of new ones; small, limited, localized, and incremental interventions or more global, comprehensive, or radical transformation**
- **adequacy of human resources: internal feasibility versus need for external consultation and funding; current faculty capabilities and interests, existing administrative personnel and support structures**

Lasting improvement of a curriculum requires what Gaff, in the context of general education, called a "more pervasive, deeper, and supportive structure." Creating an *institutional deep structure* entails five actions: shaping a new generation of faculty, developing a conducive faculty culture, building a community of learners among faculty and students, constructing shared authority, and infusing the change throughout academic departments (1991, 156). The wisest approach is not a single strategy but a portfolio of strategies that also encompasses previous strategies for faculty development, as shown in the table on page 23.

The most important consideration is ensuring that interdisciplinary studies have, as one faculty member put it, "a place at the table." They should not be extolled in institutional rhetoric but then allowed only if taught on "voluntary" overload. And, they should not be left to fend for themselves. The rhetoric of increased interdisciplinarity implies that such programs are moving to the *center* of the academy, but without support they will remain *marginal*. In order to promote greater visibility, protection, informed practices, and stimulation of new programs, interdisciplinary programs may be clustered together in an administrative office or a center. For example, the Charles Center for Honors and Interdisciplinary Studies at the College of William and Mary provides a home for interdisciplinary courses and student-developed concentrations as well as "cross-disciplinary" and "interdisciplinary" concentrations in a wide variety of fields. The center is a "hub" for interdisciplinary work and co-curricular activities on campus.

Targeting support for particular programs can be combined with general loosening of barriers. Because many disciplinary, professional, and educational organizations today encourage greater interdisciplinary activity, their reports should be read on campus to ensure that dialogue on curriculum is informed and up-to-date. Interdisciplinary activity must also be written—literally— into the deep structure of an institution, in letters of hire, tenure and promotion guidelines, and union contracts. Just as faculty should be given credit in the reward system, student accomplishments should also be recognized. Another old saw comes to mind—that interdisciplinary programs exist in the white space of organizational charts. Today, the white space is becoming more crowded, and the lines on charts are blurring. The entire "public face" of an institution should be scrutinized to insure that interdisciplinary programs are visible in all printed materials, including bulletins and catalogues. They should also be recognized in the recruitment and counseling systems. Conducting a campus-wide inventory of current interests and activities is an added step that remaps the campus by revealing and legitimating the changing landscape of higher education.

CODA: THE INTERDISCIPLINING OF THE ACADEMY

Development: Between 1875 and 1910, a "disciplining of the curriculum" occurred as the organizing principle of knowledge and higher education shifted from a single sequence of study to twenty to twenty-five disciplines—each with its own department, major, and courses. Reflecting on current trends, Douglas Bennett observed that exploration of interdisciplinary subjects presses against the disciplinary framing of the curriculum. A significant restructuring might even occur if multi- and interdisciplinary study became more thoroughgoing. Yet, nothing convinced Bennett that we are close to abandoning disciplines as the basic way of organizing knowledge and curriculum (1997, 136-37, 144-45).

SUPPORT STRATEGIES

Conduct an inventory of current interdisciplinary research and teaching interests and activities

Include interdisciplinary activities in all official materials, including course catalogues and organizational charts as well as the system of recruitment and counseling

Heed interdisciplinary recommendations of disciplinary, professional, and educational groups

Loosen structural barriers through joint appointments, cross-listing of courses, and infusing innovations and new research developments into the curriculum

Cluster dispersed programs in an interdisciplinary center or office

Recognize interdisciplinary activities in the reward system

Develop appropriate criteria for learning assessment and program review

Utilize the literatures on interdisciplinarity and consultants

Support programs by providing relevant teaching and curriculum materials.

The changes mapped in this discussion paper are the result of a widespread interdisciplining of the academy. They are not central to the academy, but neither are traditional notions of disciplinarity.

Simplified views of the system, as Burton Clark said of the modern university, only add to the problem of operational realities that outrun old expectations, especially older definitions that view one part or function of the system as its *essence* or *essential* mission (1995, 154-55). In conceptualizing what is happening, Klein and Newell (1997) turned to systems theory for a metaphor. The current extent and variety of interdisciplinary changes indicates that the structure of higher education is shifting from simple systems to complex ones. Simple systems operate according to a single set of rules, even if they have multiple levels and connections. Complex systems have multiple and conflicting logics.

In disciplines, in interdisciplinary fields, and in general education, interdisciplinary learning has become vital to preparing students to navigate a "kaleidoscopically complex world." Interdisciplinarity matters more today, because the needs it serves, while varied and even conflictual, are pervasive. "The entire ethos of the contemporary world," as Schneider and Shoenberg point out in a companion discussion paper on liberal education, "calls for the capacity to cross boundaries, explore connections, move in uncharted directions" (1997, 14-15).

Effects: The positive results of interdisciplinary studies were affirmed in recent campus-wide studies of how to improve the climate for interdisciplinary research and education (Klein 1996, 224-37). Administrators cited the flexibility to respond to new and complex needs, problems, and issues. Interdisciplinary programs enable new fields and new forms of career education. They facilitate new partnerships with the community, government, and industry. Greater recognition of interdisciplinarity also enhances an institution's ability to attract faculty in new fields, while legitimating the interdisciplinary teaching and research interests of current faculty. Moreover, it confers a unique institutional identity, an advantage in geographic areas and peer-institution networks where competition for students is keen.

Faculty cite comparable reasons. They value institutional readiness to respond to complex problems and issues as well as recognition of new research and teaching interests. They regard interdisciplinary studies as a form of faculty development, continuing education, and a counterbalance to the isolation of specialization. They associate interdisciplinarity with a capacity to promote creativity and innovation, to energize research and curriculum, to enhance communicative and collaborative skills, and to promote a greater sense of community among students and faculty alike. They also appreciate the greater legitimation an enhanced interdisciplinary climate confers on projects, teamwork, and less visible forms of integrative work they perform daily.

In addition, both administrators and faculty point to the the value of a more integrative view of knowledge and education for students. Students themselves cite a more coherent educational experience, exposure to interdisciplinary traditions and new fields, and engagement in "real world" problems and issues. Despite fears that interdisciplinary programs lessen exposure to disciplines, students report they encounter a greater variety of disciplines than they might otherwise, and they value connection making between their majors and other disciplines. Mindful of their needs as future workers and citizens, students also welcome opportunities to cultivate skills of integration and synthesis, problem solving, collaboration and teamwork, and information seeking.

Models: In the first half of the century, the defining models of interdisciplinary studies were the general education program at Columbia University and the field of American studies. The 1960s and 1970s were a watershed in the history of interdisciplinary studies. Along with new knowledge fields, new interdisciplinary institutions and cluster colleges emerged. The Evergreen State College, Hampshire College, the Hutchins School of Liberal Studies at Sonoma State University, Watauga College at Appalachian State University, and other alternative learning environments are still in place. In the late 1980s and into the 1990s, a family of movements further challenged the dominance of academic majors. In addition to reforms in general education, they included multiculturalism, feminist pedagogy, and renewed concern for the coherence of undergraduate education (Ratcliff 1997, 15).

The defining models of today encompass this history and new responses to the changing nature of knowledge and the student body. Founded in 1992, the Department of Integrative Studies at Arizona State University West seeks to reflect a twenty-first century epistemology and cultural reality. One of five interdisciplinary departments within the College of Arts and Sciences, it emphasizes focused liberal arts education through individualized programs of study and offers a major leading to a Bachelor of Arts. Elevated to "school" status in 1995, the Gallatin School at New York University offers self-designed interdisciplinary concentrations, independent studies, and internships leading to a B.A. in Individualized Study, with the option of an M.A. Founded in 1994, the new campus of California State University at Monterey Bay is organized around four learning centers and a graduate programs office. It offers twelve interdisciplinary undergraduate programs that integrate the sciences and the arts and humanities, liberal studies and professional training, modern learning technology and pedagogy, work and learning, and service and reflection. New Century College at George Mason University, established in 1995, offers coordinated-studies learning communities leading to bachelors degrees in arts or in science in Integrated Studies. Students develop their own majors or follow a specified interdisciplinary track.

The current extent and variety of interdisciplinary studies is all the more remarkable when we consider that the century began without the word "interdisciplinary" in the English language.

A BEGINNING LITERATURE FOR CAMPUSES

The majority of examples featured in this discussion paper may be found in the Edwards Directory, the Davis book, and *Handbook of the Undergraduate Curriculum*.

Davis, J. R. 1995. *Interdisciplinary courses and team teaching: New arrangements for learning*. Phoenix, AZ: American Council on Education/Oryx. The first systematic study of the topic. Includes detailed analysis of five courses from the University of Denver and descriptions of nearly 100 courses across the U.S, with information on audience, disciplines, personnel, a general description, and distinctive features.

Edwards, A.F. 1996. *Interdisciplinary undergraduate programs: A Directory*. (2nd Ed.). Acton, MA: Copley. The latest directory of programs across the U.S., with introductory reflections on the implications of the data. Each of 410 full-page descriptions includes program type, size, courses, administration, a brief narrative, and contact information.

Fiscella, J. and S. Kimmel, eds. 1998. *Interdisciplinary education: A guide to resources*. New York: The College Board. An annotated resource guide with citations from published works, associations, agencies, and electronic sources, accompanied by introductory essays organized in broad subject areas. Spans K-16.

Klein, J. T. and W. Doty, eds. 1994. *Interdisciplinary studies today*. San Francisco, CA: Jossey Bass. Number 58 (Summer) in the New Directions in Teaching and Learning series. A practical compendium of advice and information on developing courses, administering programs, assessing learning, and networking, accompanied by an introduction on finding pertinent knowledge and information,

Klein, J.T. and Newell, W.H. Advancing interdisciplinary studies. In J. Gaff and J. Ratcliff, eds. 1997. *Handbook of the undergraduate curriculum*, 393-415. A state-of-the-art account of the current nature and practices of IDS. Topics include conceptualizing IDS, forms and structures, institutional change, teaching and learning, assessment and evaluation.

Newell, W., ed. 1998. *Interdisciplinarity: Essays from the literature*. New York: The College Board. A compilation of reprinted "classic" works from varied sources, with an introduction and an analytical review of this literature focused on major topics in integration of interdisciplinary studies.

ADDITIONAL REFERENCES

AAC&U. 1990, 1991, 1992. *Liberal learning and the arts and sciences major*. 3 vols. Washington, D.C.: Association of American Colleges.

— —. 1994. *Changing the major: Innovation priorities in the fields*. Washington, D.C: AAC&U

Bennett, D. 1997. Innovation in the liberal arts and sciences. In *Education and democracy: Re-imagining liberal learning in America*, R. Orrill, ed. 131-149. New York: College Board.

Caldwell, L. 1983. Environmental studies: Discipline or metadisciplines? *Environmental Professional*, 5: 247-259.

Clark, B.R. 1995. *Places of inquiry: Research and advanced education in modern universities*. Berkeley: University of California Press.

Cornwell, G. and E. Stoddard. 1994. Things fall together: A critique of multicultural curricular reform. *Liberal Education*, 80: 4, 40-51.

Crane, D. and H. Small. 1992. American sociology since the seventies. *Sociology and its publics*, T. Halliday and M. Janowitz, eds. Chicago: University of Chicago Press, 197-234.

Field, M., R. Lee, and M.L. Field. 1994. Assessing interdisciplinary learning. In Klein and Doty 69-84,

Gaff, J. 1991. *New life for the college curriculum*. San Francisco: Jossey Bass.

Geertz, C. 1980. Blurred genres: The refiguration of social thought. *American Scholar,* 42: 4, 165-179.

Groennings, S. 1990. Higher education, international education, and the academic disciplines. In *Group portrait: Internationalizing the disciplines*, S. Groennings and D. Wiley, eds. New York: The American Forum, 11-31.

Gunn, G. 1992. Interdisciplinary studies. In *Introduction to scholarship in modern languages and literatures*, 2nd ed. J. Gibaldi, ed. New York: Modem Language Association, 239-61.

Humphreys, D. 1997. *General education and American commitments: A national report on diversity courses and requirements*. Washington, D.C.: AAC&U.

Klein, J.T. 1996. *Crossing boundaries: Knowledge, disciplinarities, and interdisciplinarities*. Charlottesville: University Press of Virginia.

Messer-Davidow, E., D. Shumway, and D. Sylvan, eds. 1993. *Knowledges: Historical and critical studies in disciplinarity*. Charlottesville: University Press of Virginia.

Minnich, E. 1995. *Liberal learning and the arts of connection for the new academy*. Washington, D.C.: AAC&U.

Musil, C. M. 1992. *Students at the center: Feminist assessment*. Washington, D.C.: AAC.

Rauch, A. 1997. Comment on interdisciplinarity. *PMLA Forum*: March, 273-274.

Schneider, Carol G., and Robert Shoenberg, 1997. *Contemporary Understandings of Liberal Education*. Washington, D.C.: AAC&U.

Stimpson, C.R. 1992. Feminist criticism. In *Redrawing the boundaries: The transformation of English and American literary studies*, S. Greenblatt and G. Gunn, eds. New York: MLA 251-270.

From forthcoming untitled book from The Evergreen Conference on Interdisciplinary Education.:

G. Cornwell and E. Stoddard, Towards an interdisciplinary epistemology: Faculty culture and institutional change

W. Newell, Integrative study

K. Schilling, Making the case for quality in programs across the street.

From Gaff, J. and J. Ratcliff. 1997. *Handbook of the undergraduate curriculum*. San Francisco: Jossey Bass.

J.T. Civian, et al., Implementing change

J. Farmer, Using technology

D.W. Farmer, E. A. Napieralski, Assessing learning in programs

J.G. Gaff, Tensions between tradition and innovation

J.G. Gaff and J. Racliff, Preface

M. Garcia and J. Ratcliff, Social forces shaping the curriculum

A.B. Hendershott and S.P. Wright, The social sciences

F.T. Janzow, J.B.. Hinni, and J. R. Johnson, Administering the curriculum

J.S. Johnston, Jr. and J. R. Spalding, Internationalizing the curriculum

J.T. Klein and W. Newell, Advancing interdisciplinary studies

R.S. Matthews, et al., Creating learning communities

C.M. Musil, Diversity and educational integrity

E. Olguin and B. Schmitz, Transforming the curriculum through diversity

J.L. Ratcliff, What is a curriculum and what should it be?

M. Reardon and J. Ramaley, Building academic community while containing costs

C.G. Schneider, The arts and sciences major

L.M. White, The humanities

G.G. Wubbels and J. S. Girgus, The natural sciences and mathematics

AAC&U Statement on Liberal Learning

A truly liberal education is one that prepares us to live responsible, productive, and creative lives in a dramatically changing world. It is an education that fosters a well grounded intellectual resilience, a disposition toward life-long learning, and an acceptance of responsibility for the ethical consequences of our ideas and actions. Liberal education requires that we understand the foundations of knowledge and inquiry about nature, culture and society; that we master core skills of perception, analysis, and expression; that we cultivate a respect for truth; that we recognize the importance of historical and cultural context; and that we explore connections among formal learning, citizenship, and service to our communities.

We experience the benefits of liberal learning by pursuing intellectual work that is honest, challenging, and significant, and by preparing ourselves to use knowledge and power in responsible ways. Liberal learning is not confined to particular fields of study. What matters in liberal education is substantial content, rigorous methodology and an active engagement with the societal, ethical, and practical implications of our learning. The spirit and value of liberal learning are equally relevant to all forms of higher education and to all students.

Because liberal learning aims to free us from the constraints of ignorance, sectarianism, and short sightedness, it prizes curiosity and seeks to expand the boundaries of human knowledge. By its nature, therefore, liberal learning is global and pluralistic. It embraces the diversity of ideas and experiences that characterize the social, natural, and intellectual world. To acknowledge such diversity in all its forms is both an intellectual commitment and a social responsibility, for nothing less will equip us to understand our world and to pursue fruitful lives.

The ability to think, to learn, and to express oneself both rigorously and creatively, the capacity to understand ideas and issues in context, the commitment to live in society, and the yearning for truth are fundamental features of our humanity. In centering education upon these qualities, liberal learning is society's best investment in our shared future.

About AAC&U

AAC&U is the leading national association devoted to providing contemporary liberal education for all students, regardless of academic specialization or intended career. Since its founding in 1915, AAC&U's membership has grown to nearly 700 accredited public and private colleges and universities of every type and size.

AAC&U functions as a catalyst and facilitator, forging links among presidents, administrators, and faculty members who are engaged in institutional and curricular planning. Its mission is to reinforce the collective commitment to liberal education at both the national and local level and to help individual institutions keep student learning at the core of their educational programs as they evolve to meet new economic and social challenges.

AAC&U's current priorities are:

Mobilizing collaborative leadership—
for educational and institutional effectiveness

Building faculty capacity—
in the context of institutional renewal

Strengthening curricula—
to serve student and societal needs

Establishing diversity—
as an educational and civic priority

Fostering global engagement—
in a diverse but connected world